Did You

EAST S

A MISCELLANY

Compiled by Julia Skinner

With particular reference to the work of Martin Andrew
and Helen Livingston

THE FRANCIS FRITH COLLECTION

www.francisfrith.com

First published in the United Kingdom in 2012 by The Francis Frith Collection®

This edition published exclusively for Bradwell Books in 2012
For trade enquiries see: www.bradwellbooks.com or tel: 0800 834 920
ISBN 978-1-84589-690-4

Text and Design copyright The Francis Frith Collection®
Photographs copyright The Francis Frith Collection® except where indicated.

The Frith® photographs and the Frith® logo are reproduced under licence from
Heritage Photographic Resources Ltd, the owners of the Frith® archive and trademarks.
'The Francis Frith Collection', 'Francis Frith' and 'Frith' are registered trademarks of
Heritage Photographic Resources Ltd.

All rights reserved. No photograph in this publication may be sold to a third party other than in the original form of this publication, or framed for sale to a third party. No parts of this publication may be reproduced, stored in a retrieval system, or transmitted, in any form, or by any means, electronic, mechanical, photocopying, recording or otherwise, without the prior permission of the publishers and copyright holder.

British Library Cataloguing in Publication Data

Did You Know? East Sussex - A Miscellany
Compiled by Julia Skinner
With particular reference to the work of Martin Andrew and Helen Livingston

The Francis Frith Collection
Oakley Business Park,
Wylye Road, Dinton,
Wiltshire SP3 5EU
Tel: +44 (0) 1722 716 376
Email: info@francisfrith.co.uk
www.francisfrith.com

Printed and bound in Malaysia
Contains material sourced from responsibly managed forests

Front Cover: **EASTBOURNE, THE PIER 1910** 62958p
Frontispiece: **BRIGHTON, FROM WEST PIER 1921** 71486
Contents: **LEWES, SOUTHOVER HIGH STREET, ANNE OF CLEVES HOUSE 1898** 41917

The colour-tinting is for illustrative purposes only, and is not intended to be historically accurate

AS WITH ANY HISTORICAL DATABASE, THE FRANCIS FRITH ARCHIVE IS CONSTANTLY BEING CORRECTED AND IMPROVED, AND THE PUBLISHERS WOULD WELCOME INFORMATION ON OMISSIONS OR INACCURACIES

CONTENTS

INTRODUCTION

In 1974 the ancient county of Sussex was divided into two new counties, East and West Sussex. The modern county of East Sussex starts just east of Brighton & Hove, and contains most of the seaside resorts of 'good old Sussex by the sea' – Hove, Brighton, Seaford, Eastbourne, Bexhill and Hastings. Here, too, are the 'ancient towns' of Rye and Winchelsea, which were important ports in the Middle Ages but are now some way inland, and the modern cross-Channel port of Newhaven. On the western side of the county are the glorious green hills of the South Downs, which culminate in spectacular style in the precipitous drop of Beachy Head, south of Eastbourne, which is the highest cliff on the south coast. The forest ridge is the high ground at the northern border of East Sussex; from it the land gradually slopes down southwards towards the Weald, a flattish region of heavy land situated between the forest ridge at the northern border of both East and West Sussex and the scarp edge of the South Downs. The Weald was heavily forested until medieval times, but is now an agricultural region of arable land.

BEACHY HEAD, FROM THE SANDS
1903 50417

STONEGATE, TICEHURST ROAD (STONEGATE) STATION 1907 58574

Brighton was the first East Sussex seaside resort to develop, in the late 18th century, and other seaside resorts were developed along the coast throughout the 19th century, their growth usually stimulated by the arrival of the railway. The arrival of the railway also helped inland towns and villages to develop or expand in the 19th century. In some places, small villages became large towns where the proximity of a station attracted new populations of residents, many of whom were commuters to London.

The settlement pattern visible on today's maps of East Sussex shows that the vast majority of the population lives beside the sea, where massive housing development has taken place along almost all the coast. Inland, although the pattern of small towns and villages has been somewhat disturbed by growth along the roads, their fundamental layout has not changed. The centres of towns like breezy hilltop Lewes and pretty Mayfield are still very recognisable in photographs over a century old.

This book takes a tour around East Sussex with photographs showing its people and places in the past, and tells some of the stories in the county's colourful and eventful history.

SUSSEX DIALECT WORDS AND PHRASES

'Allow' – to agree, or to give as an opinion – as in ***'He allowed I was right'*** – he agreed with me, or ***'He allowed the price was too high'*** – he said the price was too much.

'Ampre-ang' – toothache.

'Bawl' – to read out loud.

'Caterwise' – diagonally.

'Loving mud' – sticky mud.

'Outlandish' – foreign, a disparaging term for something not done the local way.

'Peert' – pert, lively, vivacious.

'Shuckish' or ***'shucky'*** – unsettled, changeable, as in changeable weather.

'Slub', 'slab' or ***'slob'*** – thick mud.

'Slummocky' – messy, untidy.

'Squatelings' – a disparaging term for female conversation or chatter.

'Sussex wunt be druv' – Sussex people won't be driven, or pushed around.

'Swimey' – feeling sick or faint.

'Twitten' – a narrow alleyway between hedges or buildings, short for 'betwixt and between'.

'Windogs' – clouds being blown across the sky by a strong wind.

HAUNTED EAST SUSSEX

Watchbell Street in Rye is named after the bell that hung there in medieval times and was rung to warn the town's inhabitants of imminent French raids. Watchbell Street used to be haunted by the sound of hurrying footsteps, but the steps were never heard again after an Elizabethan house in the street was bombed during the Second World War.

A famous Brighton ghost is a woman dressed in grey who is said to haunt Meeting House Lane, disappearing through an arch which was bricked up in the 19th century. Tradition says she is the ghost of a nun who was walled up alive there in medieval times after running away with her lover, but another theory is that she may have been a Quaker, as Quaker women also dressed in sober colours.

Beachy Head has a sad reputation because a number of people have committed suicide by jumping to their deaths from its high chalk cliff. Not surprisingly, several unhappy ghosts are said to haunt the area. One is a lady who walks along the cliff edge before suddenly vanishing, whilst another ghostly woman carrying a baby walks along the cliff top, then pauses at the cliff edge before stepping forward and disappearing into thin air.

Tuck's Wood, south-east of Buxted, near Uckfield, is said to haunted by the ghost of 'Nan Tuck', a woman from Rotherfield who poisoned her husband in the early 19th century. She fled the village after the murder was discovered and eventually reached the Buxted area, where she was spotted by her pursuers; she fled into the wood, where her capture seemed assured, but she had mysteriously disappeared and was never seen again. The local legend is that she died in the wood, and the spot where she expired is a bare patch of ground where no vegetation will grow, so wicked was her crime. Her unquiet ghost also haunts Nan Tuck's Lane that leads to the wood from Buxted, chasing away people who wander along the lane late at night.

EAST SUSSEX MISCELLANY

Evidence of the prehistoric period of East Sussex can be seen in the three-toed dinosaur footprints and casts preserved on rocks that are revealed at low tide along the stretch of coastline between Cooden, west of Bexhill, and Pett Level, east of Hastings.

The fossilised remains of a prehistoric forest can also be seen at very low tide on the foreshore between the footbridge at Little Galley Hill and Bulverhythe, near Bexhill. This forest was growing on part of the 'land bridge' which joined Britain and the Continent in prehistoric times, and was submerged when the sea level rose around 4,000 years ago. More remains of the drowned prehistoric forest can be seen along the foreshore between Cliff End and Winchelsea Beach, east of Hastings.

The Roman Conquest of Britain began in AD43, and the period of Roman rule over Britain lasted until the early fifth century. The Romans famously built straight roads through the countryside, and you can see part of the Roman road from London to Lewes at Holtye, in the north of the county near East Grinstead, where a small section was excavated and preserved by the Sussex Archaeological Society; it was surfaced with tons of embedded iron slag from the Roman iron works in the area.

The Romans exploited the iron-bearing sandstones of the Weald using the bloomery technique, and there was also a major ironworking site near the East Sussex coast, at Beauport Park, to the north of Hastings, which was one of the largest and most productive ironworking sites in the Roman province of Britannia. The ironworking site at Beauport was abandoned around AD250, possibly because it had become too vulnerable to the attacks of Saxon raiders.

By the late 3rd century the threat from Saxon raiders to Roman Britain was so serious that a number of defensive forts were built along the southern and eastern coastline. One of these was in East Sussex, the Roman fort of 'Anderitum', also called 'Anderidos' and 'Anderida' but known now as Pevensey Castle, which was on the coast until the sea retreated in the Middle Ages but is now half a mile inland. About two-thirds of the huge towered walls of the Roman fort still stand, and are the most awe-inspiring Roman remains in East Sussex. The Romans ended their rule over Britain in the early fifth century and withdrew their legions, leaving the Romano-British people to look to their own defences. Saxon raiding parties descended on Britain, and the 'Anglo-Saxon Chronicle' records that in the year AD491 the forces of the Saxon warlord Aelle and his son Cissa 'beset the fort of Andredesceaster [Anderitum] and slew all that were therein and not one Briton was left alive'. Many centuries later, following the Norman Conquest of 1066, William the Conqueror had a Norman castle built in a corner of the Roman fort, which also still survives, although much added to in later years. The twin-towered gateway to the castle was constructed around 1190-1220, and is one of the earliest known examples of this type.

PEVENSEY, THE CASTLE 1894 34477

In the 5th century, Saxon migrants began to settle along the wide river estuaries and numerous tidal creeks of Sussex that were very similar to their flooded homelands on the north German and Frisian coasts. Over the next few centuries these migrant settlements of initial family or tribal communities evolved into today's hamlets, villages and towns, many of which have names that betray their Saxon origins. The ending '-ing' meant 'belonging to a family or tribe'. The ending '-ton' denoted an enclosure which developed into a village. Other derivations are: '-ham', meaning 'a hamlet'; '-stead', '-stock' or 'stoke', which mean 'a place'; '-worth', meaning an enclosure; '-ley' or '-holt', meaning 'a wood'; '-den', meaning 'a valley' or 'a clearing for grazing animals'; and 'fold', meaning 'a clearing in a dense forest'. It was also these people who gave the old county of Sussex its name, recorded in the 'Anglo-Saxon Chronicle' as 'Suoseaxe', meaning 'the land of the South Saxons', which eventually became the Saxon kingdom of Sussex.

Christianity arrived later in Sussex than in many other parts of Britain, for it was not until AD681 that Wilfrid, Bishop of York and Northumbria (later canonised as St Wilfrid) came to the region on his evangelising mission to convert the South Saxon people. Fragments of Saxon handiwork occur in several East Sussex churches, including the 8th-century Bexhill Stone preserved in St Peter's Church in Bexhill, which was probably the lid to a reliquary box in which the relics of a saint were kept. The stone is decoratively carved with Celtic crosses, animals and interlace patterns, and was found in the foundations of the church when it was being renovated in 1876. The stone is presumed to date from when the first church was built on this site in the eighth century, to comply with the condition of the second Council of Nicea of AD787 that the possession of the relic of a saint or a similar holy object was necessary for the consecration of a church.

BEXHILL, ST PETER'S CHURCH, THE SAXON STONE 1894 33857

MAYFIELD, THE VILLAGE SIGN, THE DEVIL AND ST DUNSTAN c1950 M242010x

The late conflict between Christianity and paganism may be the reason for the abundance of legends about the Devil in Sussex, and one of the most famous of these is linked with Mayfield, north of Heathfield. In the 9th century the Manor of Mayfield became the property of the Archbishops of Canterbury, and St Dunstan (AD909-988), who became Archbishop of Canterbury in AD960, built an episcopal palace there called Mayfield Place, as well as founding the village and its parish church. This association has given rise to an old folktale of St Dunstan's struggle with the Devil. According to this tale, Dunstan worked for a time as a blacksmith in Mayfield, whilst spreading the Gospel. His Christian activities so enraged the Devil that he disguised himself as a beautiful young woman and attempted to seduce the holy man. Dunstan ignored the woman and kept on with his work, until he noticed a cloven hoof peeping out from beneath the woman's skirt, and realised it was the Devil in disguise. Dunstan picked up a pair of red-hot tongs from his forge and clamped them on to the Devil's nose. The Devil flew away at once, and his screams of pain could be heard from miles away. A nice finishing touch to the tale is that as the Devil flew through the sky he saw the springs of Tunbridge Wells, just over the county border in Kent, and swooped down to cool his burning nose in the water; this is why, to this day, the water from the springs there is red and tastes of sulphur. The tale is recalled in the two figures below Mayfield's town sign.

The chalk hill figure called the Long Man is cut into the slope of Windover Hill above Wilmington, north-west of Eastbourne. It is one of the largest representations of the human figure in the world, at 69.2 metres (227 feet) from head to toe, and is cleverly elongated vertically to counteract the effect of foreshortening when viewed from below the hill. It was 'discovered' in 1873 and restored, but who this mysterious giant figure represents and when it was originally cut into the turf is uncertain. Until recently it was thought to be very ancient, with the two uprights each side of the Long Man being interpreted as spears, symbols of high office, or even a doorway. However, recent archaeological research by Professor Martin Bell of Reading University suggests the figure dates from the mid 16th century and was probably laid out by monks from Wilmington Priory as a waymarker for pilgrims, depicting a pilgrim holding two walking staffs. During the Second World War the white chalk outline of the giant was painted green to camouflage it and prevent enemy aviators using it as a landmark; the figure is now marked out in white bricks.

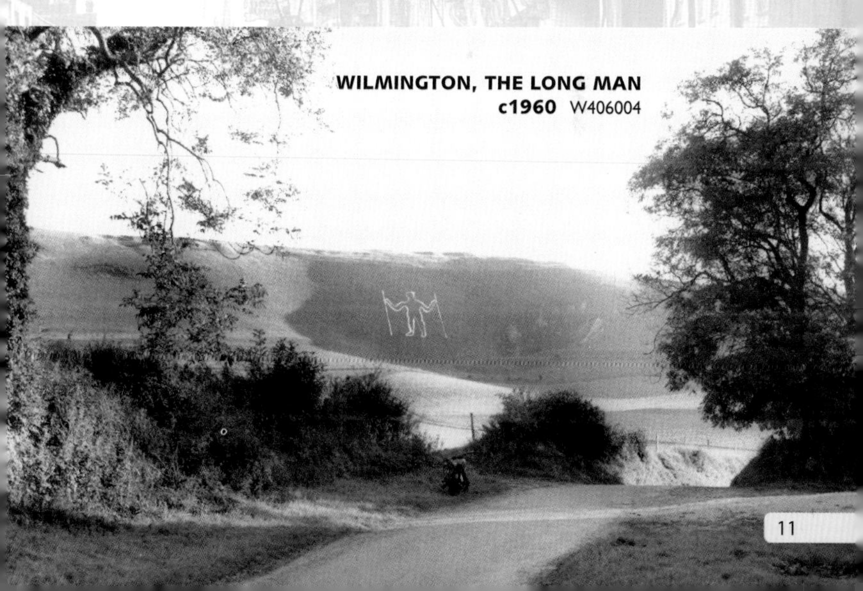

WILMINGTON, THE LONG MAN c1960 W406004

The River Cuckmere, whose Saxon name means 'flowing water', rises in the Weald near Heathfield and meanders southwards though a charming valley to enter the sea at Cuckmere Haven between Seaford Head and the Seven Sisters cliffs, which is the only river mouth in Sussex on which a port has not been built.

In the Cuckmere valley a few miles north-east of Seaford is Lullington. The tiny flint and stone Church of the Good Shepherd at Lullington, seen in this photograph, is only capable of housing some 20 worshippers and is one of the smallest churches in England. It is in fact the surviving chancel of a larger building that burned down in the 17th century.

Another notable church in this area is at Alfriston, west of Lullington and on the opposite side of the River Cuckmere. The 14th-century church of St Andrew at Alfriston is an exquisite Grade I listed building, often called 'The Cathedral of the Downs'.

LULLINGTON
THE CHURCH
1891 28396

ALFRISTON, THE VILLAGE 1921 71421

The Market Cross in the centre of Alfriston is the only original market cross remaining in East Sussex. Nearby is the Ye Olde Smugglers Inne – in the early 19th century this was the home of Stanton Collins, leader of a gang of local smugglers notorious for their violence. Alfriston's High Street is little changed today from how it looks in this 1920s view. On the right is the 14th-century George Inn, which has a number of smugglers' tunnels leading from its cellars, and on the left is the timber-framed Star Inn, one of the oldest inns in England, whose exterior is decorated with woodcarvings of beasts. The inn was originally called The Star of Bethlehem and was a hostel for pilgrims, attached to Battle Abbey, near Hastings. The former ship's figurehead in the form of a rather alarming lion seen outside the Star Inn in this view still stands outside the inn, although it has now been repositioned and painted red. It came from a Dutch warship that was wrecked off Cuckmere Haven and was brought here by Stanton Collins and his smugglers to put in front of the inn, which they used as a base.

SEAFORD, CHURCH STREET 1894 34488

The 'old town' of Seaford, centred around its medieval St Leonard's Church, used to lie at the mouth of the River Ouse and was a major port in the past, one of the medieval Confederacy of Cinque Ports of Kent and Sussex that provided ships and men for the king's navy in return for great privileges. However, the death knell was struck for the ancient port of Seaford when a storm in 1579 diverted the course of the river westward. A new port, or 'New Haven', was developed at the relocated river mouth, which is now the town of Newhaven. Seaford's fortunes revived in the 19th century, when the coming of the railway stimulated development along the seafront that made it a small seaside resort.

In past times the people of Seaford were nicknamed 'cormorants' or 'shags' (after predatory seabirds) because of their propensity for looting ships wrecked in Seaford Bay. Local legend says they were not averse to deliberately luring ships to their doom by lighting fires on the beach as false guidance lights, so they could liberate the wrecked ships of their cargoes.

Newhaven is the only port on the south coast between Dover and Portsmouth that is accessible at all states of the tide for vessels with a draught of up to four metres (13 feet).

A landmark of Newhaven is the Victorian fort built on Castle Hill to defend the harbour, one of a series of 'Palmerston Forts' constructed along the south coast in the 1860s to guard against threat of invasion by French forces. Newhaven Fort is the largest defense work ever built in Sussex, and was used for coastal defense purposes during both world wars of the 20th century. It is now preserved as an award-winning visitor attraction.

Newhaven was for a time the home of the man made famous in the song 'The Man Who Broke The Bank in Monte Carlo' – the gambler and confidence trickster Charles Deville Wells, who bought a house at 86 Fort Road with some of the proceeds of his total win of two million francs during two visits to the Monte Carlo Casino in Monaco in 1891.

NEWHAVEN, THE HARBOUR c1960 N20052

One of the most famous battles in English history took place in East Sussex on 14th October 1066, when the Anglo-Saxon forces of King Harold Godwinson fought the army of Duke William of Normandy at the Battle of Hastings. After crossing the Channel, Duke William disembarked his forces near Pevensey, which was then on the coast and not a mile inland as it is today. After laying the area waste for about 2 weeks, William and his forces marched to meet King Harold and his army on a hill about 6 miles north-west of Hastings. The Normans had the victory, and William, 'the Conqueror', became King William I. King William later founded Battle Abbey on the site of the combat, in gratitude for his victory and to atone for the slaughter, and the town of Battle grew up around it. The original Norman gatehouse of the Benedictine abbey was replaced with the magnificent gatehouse seen in this view in 1338. The abbey was dissolved by Henry VIII in 1538. The former abbot's house is now Battle Abbey School, whilst the other abbey buildings and ruins are in the care of English Heritage, with an exhibition about the battle and audio tours of the battlefield site where Anglo-Saxon England ended and the Norman Conquest of Britain began.

BATTLE, THE ABBEY GATEHOUSE 1921 71505

BODIAM CASTLE 1925 77005

The East Sussex coastline has always been susceptible to attack, and a number of Norman and medieval castles were constructed to defend its ports and rivers. One of the most spectacular castles in the county is Bodiam, which in the Middle Ages stood at the navigable limit of the River Rother. Bodiam Castle was built in 1385 against the threat of invasion by the French, following the burning of Rye in 1377 and of Winchelsea in 1380 by French raiders, and was the last medieval castle to be built in England for coastal defence.

There is also the ruined Camber Castle south of Rye, a Tudor artillery fort with graded bastions. This was one of Henry VIII's coastal defence forts that were set up all along the south coast in the 16th century. It was built to protect Rye harbour, but the sea has retreated since the fort was built in the 1540s and Camber Castle now stands in fields over a mile from the coast.

RYE
CAMBER CASTLE
1894 34446

The seaside resorts of the Sussex coast are known for their benign climate and high sunshine rate, but the Channel coast is not tame, and the prosperous and important medieval trading port of Old Winchelsea, east of Hastings, was engulfed by the sea and destroyed during severe storms in 1287. Edward I founded New Winchelsea as a hill town above its harbour in 1288, but unfortunately the harbour silted up and 'New' Winchelsea is now a mile inland. Winchelsea today has the character of an attractive village, with houses that are architecturally mostly 18th and 19th-century – but over 30 medieval undercrofts (cellars) survive beneath some of those houses, which were used for storing the Bordeaux wines that were the basis of medieval Winchelsea's trade.

This photograph shows the magnificent ash tree at Winchelsea under which John Wesley, founder of the Methodist movement of Anglican Christianity, preached his last open air sermon on 7th October 1790, six months before his death. The Wesley Tree blew down during a storm in 1927 but was replaced with a cutting from the original tree, which grew into the fine ash tree that stands in Winchelsea today.

WINCHELSEA, THE WESLEY TREE 1912 64938

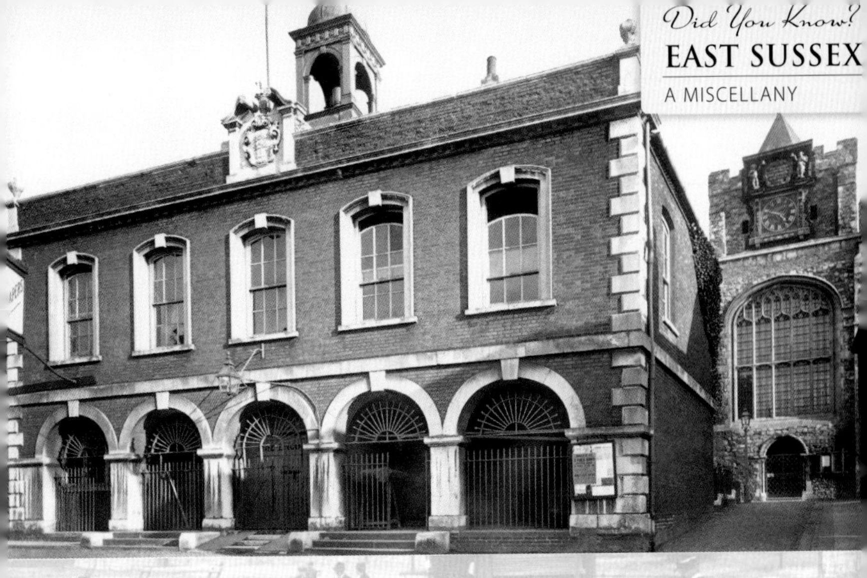

RYE, THE TOWN HALL AND ST MARY'S CHURCH 1901 47459

Rye used to be an important port, but the sea has retreated over the years and it is now some two miles inland. On Mayoring Day the new mayor throws heated coins from an upper window of Rye's Town Hall to children waiting below, an event known as 'hot-penny scramble', which commemorates when coins were minted in the town. Several relics from Rye's past are preserved inside the Town Hall, including the Rye Gibbet Cage which contains the skull of its last victim, a local butcher called John Breads, who was hanged for murder in 1742 and his remains exposed in the cage on Gibbet Marsh. He had intended to kill the town's mayor, Thomas Lamb, but in an unfortunate case of mistaken identity his victim was another man, Allan Grebell, who had borrowed a cloak from Mr Lamb after visiting him at his home. The inscription on Mr Grebell's grave-slab in the floor of St Mary's Church near the Town Hall records how he 'fell by the cruel stab of a sanguinary butcher'. The clock on St Mary's Church in Rye, seen in this view, is the oldest church turret clock in England still working with its original mechanism, and was installed in the church around 1561-2. The present exterior clock face and the two 'Quarter Boys' that strike the hours were added in 1760.

One of Europe's largest beach-launched fishing fleets operates out of Hastings. The boats are pushed by tractors across the shingle at the eastern end of the beach to be launched at high tide, then winched back onto the beach on their return. Hastings is famous for the unique tall weather-boarded net-drying sheds clustered beneath East Cliff, where fishermen used to keep their tackle and dry and store their nets. There are now 43 net 'shops', but there used to be over 100. They were built tall and thin so as many fishermen as possible could have a shed on the limited space, and also to save money, since the fishermen had to pay ground rent on the space they occupied.

Hastings and Brighton are amongst the few places in Britain that still observe an annual religious ceremony to mark the start of the local fishing season. In Hastings the ceremony is called Blessing the Sea and is held near the Lifeboat Station on the beach; sea-themed hymns are sung, and a collection is made for the local Lifeboat crew. At Brighton, the ceremony is called the Blessing of the Nets and is part of the annual Mackerel Fayre held in the Fishing Quarter surrounding the Fishing Museum near Brighton Pier.

HASTINGS
THE LIFEBOAT HOUSE AND FISHERMEN'S HUTS
1894 34427

St Clement's Church in Hastings Old Town has two strange round objects set into the stonework of the wall each side of the belfry louvre of its tower. One is a cannon-ball which was fired at the church from a ship offshore several hundred years ago and embedded itself into the stonework; the other round object is made of stone and was added to the tower many years later, in the cause of symmetry!

The 'Television Age' was born in Hastings in the 1920s. The television pioneer John Logie Baird (1888-1946) came to lodge at 21 Linton Crescent in the town in late 1922 to recuperate after an illness, and stayed until 1924. To pass the time he picked up his earlier experimental work on what he called 'Seeing by Wireless'. As well as working at 21 Linton Crescent, he also set up a laboratory over a shop at 8 Queens Arcade in the town. It was at Hastings in 1923 that he built the world's first primitive working television set and transmitted the first televised image, of his assistant's hand. In January 1924 it was also in Hastings that he gave the first public demonstration of television, transmitting images of the Maltese Cross on a St John's Ambulance Medal. Exhibits and archive information about Baird's work can be seen in Hastings Museum.

St Leonards-on-Sea, west of Hastings, was originally developed by the architect and builder James Burton and laid out between 1826 and 1837 as the first purpose-built seaside resort in the country. His son, Decimus Burton, continued developing the town after James Burton died in 1837. James Burton built himself a house on the seafront that was then called West Villa, but is now the Crown House pub at 57 Marina, and one of the town's most important historic buildings; the timber frame for the house was constructed in London and brought to St Leonards by sea. Another of James Burton's surviving buildings in the town is North Lodge that spans Upper Maze Hill, designed in mock Gothic style as a tollgate for the toll road that ran from here to join the London to Hastings Road. From 1918 until 1923 North Lodge was the home of the author Sir Henry Rider Haggard, who wrote 'King Solomon's Mines' and 'She'.

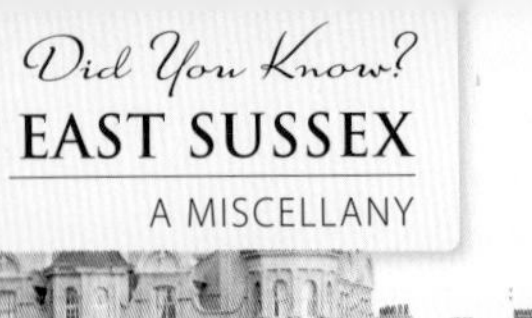

BEXHILL, THE PARADE 1903 50305

The seaside resort of Bexhill did not really develop until the late 19th century, initiated by the 7th Earl De La Warr, the lord of the manor. Despite Bexhill's growth, the 'old town' on the hill still remains a charming part of the town. In the 1890s photograph of Old Bexhill on the opposite page we are looking down Church Street, with the Bell Hotel on the left. The walnut tree on the right of this view once marked Bexhill's town centre. The tree was cut down in 1921, but still plays a part in Bexhill life – the gavel used to keep order at local council meetings was turned from a piece of wood taken from the tree.

The 1930s' De La Warr Pavilion on Bexhill's seafront is widely considered to be one of the architectural gems of the south coast, designed in International Modern style by the German architects Erich Mondelsohn and Serge Chermayeff. It was the first public building in the country to have a welded steel frame. It was constructed as an entertainment centre and opened in 1936.

BEXHILL, THE OLD TOWN, THE WALNUT TREE 1897 38994

In 1902 the first motor-racing trials in England were held at Bexhill, on a course leading from Galley Hill to the De La Warr Parade. A marker showing the beginning of that early motor racing track can be found just west of Galley Hill.

BEXHILL, THE DE LA WARR PAVILION c1965 B81046

A relic of crime and punishment in bygone times can be seen at Ninfield, north of Bexhill, where a set of stocks and a whipping post stand on the village green. Stocks were generally made of wood, but Ninfield's are unusual as they are made of iron, a refection of the village's involvement in the Sussex iron industry of the past (see page 41). In 1790 Ninfield's village green was the scene of a wife-sale, when a man sold his wife for half a pint of gin. A contemporary account was recorded in 'The Historical Magazine, or Classical Library of Public Events', volume 2, for the year 1790: 'A man at Ninfield stocks in Sussex, latterly sold his wife to another man of the same place for the valuable commodity of half a pint of gin; but the buyer being in liquor, and the seller wishing to take no unfair advantage of him, consented not to take her to bed and board till the next morning, when the purchaser attended to receive her, and to whom she was delivered with a halter about her neck in the presence of two witnesses. She appeared mightily delighted with the ceremony, which being over, the hopeful pair departed, filled with joy and expectation from the happy union.' Sadly, this story does not have the happy ending the lady seemed to be hoping for – her legal husband later changed his mind and bought her back, although her value had gone up in the meantime and he had to pay 'an advanced price'.

West of Ninfield is Herstmonceux, home of the famous Truggery where traditional Sussex trugs are still made. Much used by gardeners, Sussex trugs are wide, flat baskets made from thin slats of sweet chestnut and willow, pared off the wood with a drawknife. Most trugs have wooden feet and a handle made with a strip of wood. They are renowned for their strength and durability and became very popular in the 19th century after Thomas Smith of Herstmonceux exhibited his trugs at the Great Exhibition of 1851, where he won a gold medal and was honoured with an order by Queen Victoria.

The magnificent moated Herstmonceux Castle is seen in its romantic ruin phase in this photograph, which lasted from 1777 (when the interior was removed to build Herstmonceux Place, a mile away) until 1911, when it was restored. The castle forms part of the oldest brick mansion in Britain; in the 1440s Roger de Fiennes was granted a royal licence to 'embattle' (fortify) his manor house at Herstmonceux and it was rebuilt in a military style using locally made brick. The castle is now a beautiful mellow red and is used as an International Study Centre and events venue. The grounds of Herstmonceux Castle were the home of the Royal Greenwich Observatory from 1957 until 1988. Several telescopes still stand in the grounds, although only the dome of the largest remains, the Isaac Newton Telescope that was moved to the Canary Islands in the 1970s, and form part of The Observatory Science Centre, an educational facility with a range of exhibits, activities and science shows.

During the First World War, the War Secretary Lord Kitchener famously appealed to men to enlist. Colonel Claude Lowther of Herstmonceux Castle responded by forming a county-wide committee to raise men for the Royal Sussex Regiment. These volunteers were known as the Southdown Battalions, and the men were called the 'Southdowners' or 'Lowther's Lambs', after the famous Southdown sheep of Sussex.

HERSTMONCEUX CASTLE, THE WEST FRONT
1890 25345

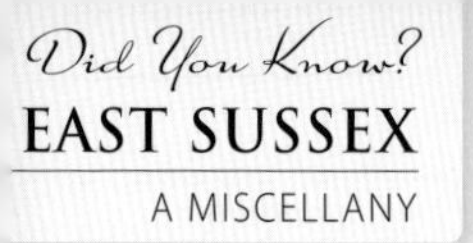

Hailsham lies seven miles north of Eastbourne on the western edge of the Pevensey Levels, an area of former sea marsh that stretches eastward for about eight miles towards Bexhill. In Roman times the Levels were part of the sea, but shingle banks cut this area off from the coast during Anglo-Saxon times and it became salt marsh. Over time the Levels gradually changed from salt marsh to reed beds and sedge meadows, and the reeds and hemp grown there produced the raw materials for the rope- and twine-making industry that for many years was Hailsham's main business, giving it the nickname of 'String Town'.

Hailsham's rope- and twine-making industry was started by Thomas Burfield, who arrived in the town around 1780 as an itinerant saddler and horse-collar maker. He started a saddlery business in the High Street in 1807, and soon diversified in rope, twine and string making, building factories in South Road which incorporated immensely long rope walks where the hemp was twisted into ropes. Besides Burfield & Sons, many other rope walks and rope works were established in Hailsham, including Green Brothers on Summerheath Road. Other works were situated behind the Crown and 89 South Street, in Stoney Lane, in Mill Road, in Bell Banks and in Common Road. By the 1880s, Burfield & Sons and Green Brothers (founded by George Green, a yarn spinner at Burfields who set up on his own) each employed over 200 hands. Green Brothers had the dubious honour of making official hangmen's ropes. All the rope works diversified into similar related products such as hop pockets, sacking, mill sails and whipcord, while during the Second World War Green Brothers made camouflage netting, sails, aeroplane hangar covers and even 500 dummy aircraft to confuse German air reconnaissance. The rope works have now gone, but Burfield & Sons' factories on South Road are perpetuated in the name of Burfield Park Industrial Estate, and Green Brothers' Summerheath Road factory in the names of the closes of modern houses, Rope Walk and Green Grove.

In the early 19th century a number of defensive structures were constructed along the East Sussex coast to counter the imminent threat of invasion by the forces of Napoleon Bonaparte of France. The flat, exposed coastline of Kent and the eastern side of East Sussex was protected by the construction of the 28-mile-long Royal Military Canal from Seabrook in Kent to Cliff End, east of Hastings, in East Sussex. The canal's function was to be an obstacle for invaders and also a means of transport for goods, supplies and troops. It is now an attractive feature in the landscape.

Further defences against Napoleon's forces included a chain of 74 forts called Martello Towers constructed along the coast from Folkestone in Kent to Seaford in East Sussex. Named after a formidable fortification on Mortella Point on Corsica, these round, squat towers with extremely thick walls were massively strong. On the roof of each tower was a 24-pounder cannon with a range of 1,000 yards, mounted on a pivot so it could rotate through 360 degrees. Most Martello Towers have been lost to coastal erosion or destroyed, but some of the survivors have been turned into houses, such as number 55 at Norman's Bay and number 60 at Pevensey Bay, or museums, such as number 74 at Seaford, and number 73 at Eastbourne, known as the Wish Tower (seen in the distance on the left of photograph 56684 on page 28). The first tower in the line along the East Sussex coast, number 28, also still stands on the west bank of the River Rother in Rye harbour, at the entrance to Frenchman's Beach Holiday Park. None of the Martello Towers ever saw action, as Napoleon Bonaparte eventually turned his attention away from invading England to deal with Austria. Perhaps he had heard about the reception he could expect if he dared to emulate William the Conqueror and land his army on the East Sussex coast – as an old rhyme put it:

'If Boneyparte should have the heart
To land on Pens'ny Levels,
Then English sons with English guns
Will blow him to the Devil.'

EASTBOURNE, FROM THE PIER 1906 56684

The Old Town of Eastbourne is a mile inland from the coast, and was engulfed by the seaside resort that grew rapidly after 1849 when the railway was allowed in by the major local landowner, William Cavendish, 2nd Earl of Burlington, who became the 7th Duke of Devonshire in 1858. The Duke developed his estates at Eastbourne into a huge resort with nearly three miles of seafront, and his ownership of so much of the town allowed for carefully controlled architecture in a classical style. Eastbourne's Grand Parade along the seafront has been described as 'one of the finest of its kind in England'. By the 1880s elegant, stylish Eastbourne had become known as 'the Empress of Watering Places'.

The chalk cliff of Beachy Head is the highest on the south coast, and this headland is sometimes called 'the lion of Eastbourne' as it guards the town from the worst of the westerly winds that blow along the coast. This is one of the reasons why Mediterranean plants such as Agapanthus can bloom along the seafront. Eastbourne's Promenade is also enhanced by the famous Carpet Gardens that form its colourful centrepiece. An average total of 39,000 seasonal spring and summer plants and 32,600 carpet bedding plants are used to plant the flower beds each year.

Eastbourne's pier, designed by Eugenius Birch, opened in 1872. The first pierhead pavilion at the seaward end was built in 1888 and was rebuilt in 1899, replete with a busy café and offices as well as a famous 360-degree Camera Obscura in the dome, which revolved on huge ball-bearings. A silver-surfaced mirror mounted at 45 degrees picked up the image of the outside scene and projected it onto a white painted screen. The Camera Obscura fell into disuse in the 1960s but was restored in 2003, and Eastbourne Pier is now the only pier in the world to have a fully functioning Victorian projector of this type.

The 1930s' bandstand on Eastbourne's seafront has a unique semi-circular design and blue-domed roof, the only such example in the country. On the promenade opposite the bandstand is a memorial plaque to former Eastbourne resident John Wesley Woodward, who was a cello player in the Eastbourne Municipal Orchestra, the Duke of Devonshire's Orchestra and the Grand Hotel, Eastbourne, Orchestra before joining the orchestra of the ill-fated 'Titanic' that sank in April 1912 after hitting an iceberg; the courageous members of the orchestra famously kept playing as the liner went down in an effort to restore calm to the desperate scene, and perished with the ship. The memorial plaque was restored and rededicated in April 2012, the centenary year of the disaster.

EASTBOURNE, THE PIER
1925 77946

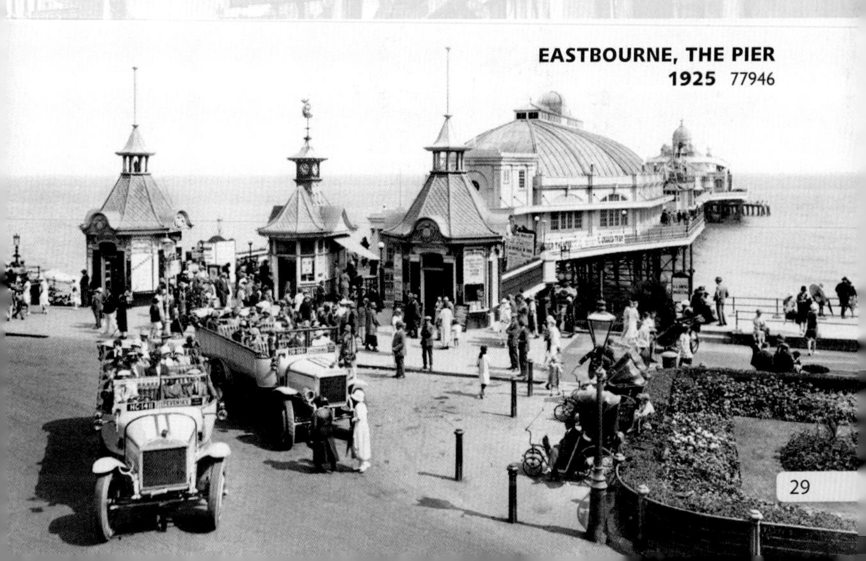

The county town of East Sussex is Lewes, dominated by its castle built to guard the gap through the Downs cut by the River Ouse, though all that remains today is the great keep, the 11th-century gateway and the 14th-century barbican arch. Lewes Castle is one of only two castles in England to have two 'mottes', or mounds, the other being Lincoln Castle. The Bull House Café on the right of this view of Lewes High Street is a 15th-century building that was originally the Bull Inn; the part set back from the High Street and accessed via Bull Lane was built later, in the 1580s, and the overhang of its upper storey is supported by two unusual jetty brackets in the form of carved wooden satyrs, mythological creatures with the body and head of a human, but the legs of a goat. From 1768 to 1774 Bull House was the home of Thomas Paine, the radical philosopher and author of the influential books 'The Rights of Man', 'The Age of Reason', and 'Common Sense', who lodged there whilst working as an excise man based at Newhaven, and married the landlord's daughter. He spent many evenings at the White Hart Hotel in the town taking part in political debates with the Headstrong Club before going off to join the American and French revolutions that his writings did much to inspire.

LEWES, HIGH STREET c1955 L40078

The walls of many buildings in Lewes are covered in 'mathematical tiles' which look like bricks but are in fact red and black tiles, sometimes glazed, and fixed to flat pieces of wood. Mathematical tiles were introduced in 1796 to avoid paying a tax on bricks and were used to give a fashionable brick-built appearance to an older timber-framed structure.

One of the best timber-framed houses in Lewes is Anne of Cleves House in Southover High Street, seen in the photograph on the contents page of this book. The house was given to Anne of Cleves, Henry VIII's fourth wife, as part of her divorce settlement in 1538, but she never actually lived there. It is now used as a museum, with rooms furnished in period style, a collection of Sussex cast iron work, carved stone from St Pancras Priory, musical instruments and a social history gallery.

On the south side of the chancel in St Anne's Church in Lewes is a small window, or 'squint', through which you can see the remains of a small cell where a holy woman known as an anchoress allowed herself to be walled up in the Middle Ages to spend her days praying for the community in return for sustenance. She could watch services and receive the Sacrament through the squint, but was not allowed to ever leave her cell – in fact, she was buried there after her death, but her remains were found in 1927 and were reburied in the churchyard.

South Street in Lewes was the scene of tragedy on 27th December 1836, when an avalanche of snow crashed down from the cliffs above and buried seven cottages – eight people died. The disaster is commemorated in the name of The Snowdrop Inn.

Many years ago fishwives from Brighton used to walk to Lewes along the old medieval drove road over the Downs, carrying their wares in wide, circular baskets known as 'juggs'; these baskets are recalled in the names of Juggs Road on the outskirts of Lewes and Juggs Lane and the Juggs Arms pub in the nearby village of Kingston, where the pub sign depicts a woman packing fish into a 'jugg'.

Brighton was originally a fishing village called Brighthelmstone, bounded by West Street, East Street and North Street, the area of town now known as 'The Lanes'. There was once a South Street, and indeed a whole 'lower town' on the beach, but they were both engulfed by the sea in the early 18th century.

Brighton's fortunes changed after a Lewes doctor, Richard Russell, moved there in 1754 to supervise his sea water cures, for glandular diseases in particular, and published a treatise on the beneficial effects of sea water. Dr Russell recommended not only sea bathing but also that sea water should be drunk, hot with a little milk or cream of tartar, an idea that, amazingly, caught on with fashionable society. Brighton's success as a centre of fun and fashion was cemented by the patronage of the Prince of Wales, who became Prince Regent in 1811 and George IV in 1820. Prince George made his first visit to Brighton in 1783 at the age of 21 and was delighted with the place. He secretly (and illegally) married the Roman Catholic Maria Fitzherbert in 1785, who lived in a villa in Brighton, and took a lease on a 'superior farmhouse' to be near her. Over the following years the prince spent much of his leisure time in Brighton and developed his residence there into the extraordinary Royal Pavilion, transformed by John Nash between 1813 and 1822 into a romantic fantasy palace bedecked with domes and minarets in a hybrid of Indian/Turkish/Arabic style.

When Queen Victoria came to the throne she disliked the Royal Pavilion for its lack of privacy, especially after the opening of the London to Brighton Railway in 1841 changed Brighton from a select watering place into a centre of mass entertainment. The Royal Pavilion was bought for the people of Brighton by the Town Commissioners, and stands today as a monument to George IV's notorious extravagance. The spectacular 18th-century 'chinoiserie' décor inside the Pavilion has been beautifully preserved, and the kitchens are of particular interest, where the celebrated chef Marie-Antoine Carême, the 'King of Chefs, and the Chef of Kings', worked for a while for George IV.

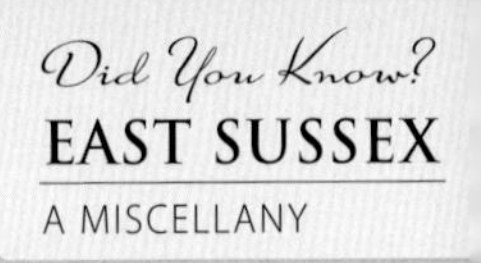

Brighton obviously had a risqué reputation in Jane Austen's day. In her novel 'Pride and Prejudice', published in 1813, Elizabeth Bennet begs her father not to allow her younger sister Lydia to go to Brighton, fearing she will be led astray by the company she will meet there. Her advice is ignored, resulting in Lydia's scandalous elopement with Wickham. Whatever would Jane Austen have made of Brighton becoming the first major resort in the country to sanction a naturist beach, in 1980, at Cliff bathing beach below Duke's Mound!

St Nicholas's Church in Dyke Road is the oldest building in Brighton, and was probably built on a hill so a fire could be lit on the flat church tower to act as a beacon to mariners, especially as the dedication of the church is to St Nicholas of Myra, the patron saint of fishermen and sailors. The church is noteworthy for its beautiful Norman font of Caen stone, carved with scenes of the baptism of Christ, the Last Supper and the legend of St Nicholas.

BRIGHTON, THE ROYAL PAVILION 1889 22244

The photograph on the title page of this book shows a view of Brighton from West Pier, which was built in the 1860s to designs by Eugenius Birch and embellished over the years. Sadly it declined in the second half of the 20th century and its derelict remains were destroyed by fire in 2003. However, Brighton's Palace Pier still stands and remains a popular feature of the town, although it is now called Brighton Pier. On the right of the photograph are two of Brighton's famous seafront hotels. The prominent building right of centre, with flags flying from its roof, is the Hotel Metropole, designed by Alfred Waterhouse, which was the largest hotel outside London when it opened in 1890; on the extreme right is the Grand Hotel, which was badly damaged by a terrorist bomb in 1984 during the Conservative Party conference, but has been restored to its former glory.

Brighton acquired the first public electric railway in the country in 1883 when Magnus Volk's seafront line opened. It still runs along the seashore in summer, between Black Rock and Brighton Pier.

The 19th-century author Lewis Carroll (real name Charles Dodgson) visited Brighton many times, as his sister lived at 11 Sussex Square from 1874 until 1887. The private tunnel from Sussex Square Gardens that runs under the coast road down to the beach may have been the inspiration for the opening chapter of his most famous work, 'Alice's Adventures in Wonderland', when Alice follows the White Rabbit down the rabbit hole into Wonderland.

In the 1960s Brighton was the scene of several clashes between the rival youth culture gangs known as the 'mods' and the 'rockers'. The worst clash was on 17th and 18th May 1964, when 3,000 youths fought in the town. The incident was made the subject of a feature film, 'Quadrophenia', in 1970, much of which was filmed on location in Brighton. The name comes from the album 'Quadrophenia' by The Who; this now-legendary supergroup was the resident band in The Florida Rooms in Brighton in the 1960s.

Hove developed to the west of Brighton after the waters of St Ann's Well, a chalybeate (iron-bearing) spring in St Ann's Well Gardens, were also recommended by Dr Russell in his treatise of the 1750s that made Brighton popular. Behind the promenade in this view are the superb compositions of Brunswick Square, Brunswick Terrace (perhaps the most magnificent Regency development in Britain) and Adelaide Terrace beyond.

One of the treasures in Hove Museum in New Church Road is the Hove amber cup. This was found in an oak coffin in a Bronze Age burial mound in the 1850s when work was underway to create Palmeira Square, along with a stone axe-head, a whetstone and a bronze dagger. The cup is nearly 7cms (3 inches) high, and was turned on a lathe from a single block of red Baltic amber. The Hove Cup is approximately 3,200 years old and one of Britain's most important Bronze Age finds.

Brighton and Hove merged to form the borough of Brighton & Hove in 1997, and the unitary borough was granted city status as part of the Millennium celebrations in 2000.

HOVE, THE PARADE 1921 71501

East of Brighton along the coast is Rottingdean. During the Victorian period many writers and artists were drawn to live in Rottingdean by the tranquil atmosphere of the village, including the poet and author Rudyard Kipling (1865-1936). Kipling lived in The Elms at the centre of The Green at Rottingdean from 1897 until 1903, when sightseers drove him away to a more private home in East Sussex at Batemans, a fine Jacobean house near Burwash that is now in the care of the National Trust. Whilst he lived at Rottingdean, the Downs around the village inspired Kipling's poem 'Sussex' of 1902, in which he famously summed up the magnificent downland landscape of East Sussex in a single line: 'Our blunt, bow-headed, whale-backed Downs'. Built into the eastern wall surrounding Kipling's former home of The Elms at Rottingdean, just south of the Dean Court Road junction and about six feet from the ground, is a strange stone carved in the shape of a head, which was formerly in the churchyard. This is a 'wishing stone', and local legend says that anyone who strokes the nose of the head gently in a clockwise motion with the forefinger of the right hand and then turns around three times will be granted their dearest wish.

A short distance east of Rottingdean is Piddinghoe, in the Ouse valley. St John's Church in Piddinghoe is famous for its flint-built round tower, one of the three Norman round towers of Sussex – the other two are St Peter's Church at Southease, a short distance north of Piddinghoe, and St Michael's Church in Lewes. No one knows for sure why these towers are round, but they were probably constructed this way because of the difficulty of making corners out of flint. Piddinghoe's church tower is surmounted with a shingled octagonal spire topped with a weathervane in the shape of a fish – this was famously mentioned in Rudyard Kipling's poem 'Sussex' as 'Where windy Piddinghoe's begilded dolphin veers', but the fish is actually a depiction of a sea trout or salmon, not a dolphin.

Alciston is off the A27 between Eastbourne and Lewes. There is a 16th-century tithe barn in the village which at 52 metres (170 feet) long is the largest example in Sussex, and one of the longest in the country. Alciston was a grange of Battle Abbey, and the barn was used for storing the tithes (a tenth of the produce of local farms) which had to be given to the Church. Alciston is also famous for the annual 'Long Rope' skipping contest that takes place every Good Friday on the closed-off road outside the Rose Cottage Inn, a colourful event that also includes traditional music and morris dancing. Skipping used to be a traditional Easter custom in a number of places in England on Good Friday, which was also known as Long Rope Day or Long Line Day. The custom may have originated in coastal areas, when fishermen sorted out their ropes for the start of the fishing season, discarded any that were past their prime and used them for skipping, with the rope representing the one that Judas Iscariot hanged himself with after betraying Jesus. In Brighton, local fishermen used to skip in the fish market on Good Friday. Alciston is now the only place in East Sussex where the Good Friday skipping tradition continues.

Glynde, east of Lewes, has a gem of a small 18th-century church in its parish church of St Mary the Virgin, something quite rare in Sussex. This delightfully elegant building in Palladian style stands alongside Glynde Place and was built in 1763 of knapped flints. The interior is unusual, as the walls of the church are faced with printed hessian fabric.

North of Glynde on the B2192 is Ringmer, where the village sign features an unexpected sight – a tortoise. This represents Timothy the Tortoise (actually a female of the species) who belonged to Ringmer resident Rebecca Snooke in the 18th century. Rebecca, who lived at Delves House, was the aunt of the famous naturalist Gilbert White, who visited his aunt regularly and made a study of Timothy, recording his observations in his letters and journal. Gilbert White took Timothy to live with him at his home in Selborne in Hampshire after his aunt died, where he continued to study the tortoise's habits. Timothy's shell is now preserved in the Natural History Museum in Kensington.

TICEHURST, THE VILLAGE AND THE CHURCH 1903 49352

In ancient times the great primeval forest of 'Andreadswald' covered much of Kent, Surrey and Sussex and gave its name to the Weald, a flattish region of heavy land between the forest ridge at the northern border of Sussex and the South Downs. The Weald remained heavily forested and was not perceived as an area to be farmed until the Middle Ages, with only a few small clearings made in the woodland for habitation – the 'hursts' of the region, such as Ticehurst and Wadhurst – but is now an agricultural region.

The remains of the huge Wealden forest of the past are now split up into separate patches of woodland in both East and West Sussex. Ashdown Forest in the north-west corner of East Sussex is the largest, and includes tracts of heath, moorland and rocky outcrops as well as woodland. Many of the forest hamlets, such as Chelwood Gate and Coleman's Hatch, take their names from the old 'hatches' or gates into the forest in past times.

Forest Row is also named from its proximity to Ashdown Forest. Nowadays the beauty of the countryside in this region is much appreciated, but it was not always so. The writer William Cobbett travelled from Forest Row to Uckfield in 1822, and famously described Ashdown Forest in his 'Rural Rides' as 'a heath with here and there a few birch scrubs upon it, verily the most villainously ugly spot I ever saw in England'.

East of Forest Row is Hartfield, which is famous for its connections with Winnie-the-Pooh – the much-loved fictional bear 'with very little brain'. Pooh Bear was the creation of the author A A Milne who lived at Cotchford Farm near Hartfield for many years. The nearby Five Hundred Acre Wood of Ashdown Forest inspired the Hundred Acre Wood of his books in which Winnie-the-Pooh and his friends lived and had their adventures, and E H Shepherd based many of his delightful illustrations for the books on the actual locations in the area that A A Milne had in mind, including the small wooden bridge spanning the Posingford Stream in Posingford Wood, south of Harting, where Christopher Robin and Pooh played 'poohsticks'. A path leads through Posingford Wood to the bridge from the Pooh Bridge Car Park, found by turning off the B2026 into Chuck House Lane, following the signpost to Marsh Green and Newbridge – the car park is just along the lane on the right.

FOREST ROW, THE VILLAGE 1902 48265

Crowborough is the highest town in East Sussex, and in the early 1900s was being promoted by local estate agents as 'Scotland in Sussex'! Crowborough was just a small village until local resident Dr Prince persuaded Lord Abergavenny, the major landowner, that the area's healthy air and scenic location made it ideal for people suffering from 'diseases of the respiratory organs, nervous depression, languor and debility of the systems', and it was laid out in the 1870s as a health resort with avenues of detached villas. It grew even more after the railway arrived, and became an early commuter town. This photograph shows what used to be called the Red Cross Hotel at Crowborough Cross, now the Crowborough Cross pub in Beacon Road. The inn dates from the 17th century, and its original name probably derived from the red cross placed on coaching maps to denote Crowborough Cross for illiterate coachmen. Opposite the pub is Cloke's Corner, where a famous past resident of the town is commemorated with a bronze statue by local sculptor David Cornell – the author Sir Arthur Conan Doyle, creator of Sherlock Holmes, who lived at what is now called Windlesham Manor on the outskirts of Crowborough from 1907 until his death in 1930.

CROWBOROUGH, THE RED CROSS HOTEL 1900 44949

The deposits of iron ore in the Wealden sandstones allowed an important iron industry to flourish in a number of towns and villages of Sussex in the past, which predated the use of coal for smelting iron – the fuel used was charcoal, made by coppicing trees in local woods and forests. The introduction of water-powered bloomery forges in the 15th century revolutionised the industry. Furnaces and forges were sited beside streams whose water was diverted and contained by dams to create furnace ponds to drive waterwheels powering the furnace bellows, and hammer ponds to drive waterwheels powering huge forging hammers used for working the iron. A major name in the history of the iron industry was William Levett (c1495-1554), who as well as being rector of Buxted, near Uckfield, also had an interest in the emerging English armaments industry. He was a pivotal figure in the use of the blast furnace to manufacture iron and owned a number of iron furnaces in East Sussex. The first cast-iron muzzle-loader cannon cast in England was produced in 1543 at Buxted by two of his employees, Ralph Hogge and French-born master gun-founder Pierre Baude. Following Reverend Levett's death in 1554, Ralph Hogge carried on the manufacture of iron in his own right, becoming a major ironmaster who operated a number of furnaces and forges in the area around Uckfield. His rebus, or personal stamp, of a hog (a pig) features on Buxted's village sign, as well as one of the cannons that were turned out in huge numbers by the Sussex iron industry in the 16th and 17th century and were its most important products. An example of a Sussex-made cannon, a demi-culverin, can be seen today at Pevensey Castle.

The Sussex iron industry came to an end when coal-fired blast furnaces were introduced in the mid 18th-century, making iron production easier and cheaper, and the iron industry moved to the north of England, to be nearer the supply of coal. All that is left now of this once-important industry are some of the iron-works ponds created to power the workings; although many of the old furnace and hammer ponds are now dry, those that remain form beautiful features of the landscape.

UCKFIELD, HIGH STREET 1904 52911

Uckfield was a centre of the Sussex iron industry in the 17th and 18th centuries, and was also well-known for its brickworks into the 20th century. The oldest house in the town is the picturesque timber-framed Bridge Cottage in the High Street, a 15th-century Wealden hall house that is now the headquarters of the Uckfield and District Preservation Society. An intriguing street name in Uckfield is Pudding Cake Lane that runs off Church Street, which got its name from the pudding cake that in past times was a popular delicacy served in a pub sited in the lane.

Uckfield's Roman Catholic Church of Our Lady and St Philip Neri in the High Street is a striking modern building that was consecrated in 1961. On the frontage of its tower is a most unusual bronze statue by Marcus Cornish of a halo-ed Jesus in modern clothes, wearing a short-sleeved shirt and baggy trousers. Dubbed 'Jesus in Jeans', the statue was chosen after a vote by the church's congregation and unveiled in 2009. It provides a welcoming and dynamic view of Christ for the 21st century.

Along the A22 from the north-western corner of East Sussex down to Eastbourne and on the A26 from Uckfield to Lewes are a series of milestones that were erected after these routes were constructed as turnpike roads in the 18th century, built by Turnpike Trusts that charged tolls from travellers using the roads. Milestones were usually made from stone, but these are unusual because they are made of cast iron – and Sussex iron at that. Each milestone was cast with the symbols of a bow of ribbon above a string of bells, above which is a number referring to the mileage from that point to the door of the church of St-Mary-le-Bow in the City of London – the symbols represent the church's famous Bow Bells. The milestones from the 44 to 54 mile points along the Uckfield to Horsebridge route along the A22 are also topped with a Pelham Buckle above the bow, which was the symbol of the Pelham family, the landowners of the area who lived in Halland at the time and were involved in financially backing this section of the turnpike road in the 1750s. The Pelham Buckle emblem can also be seen in many churches of the area; it dates from 1356, when Sir John Pelham helped capture the King of France at the Battle of Poitiers and was given the king's belt buckle as a badge of honour.

East of Uckfield is Heathfield, where in the late 18th and early 19th centuries Jonathan Harmer made glazed terracotta bas-relief plaques that he set into shallow cavities on gravestones as decorative embellishments, using a special mortar. He made them in a range of designs, including urns, winged cherubs, vases of flowers and baskets of fruit, and in colours ranging from cream to orangey-red. Jonathan died in 1839, taking the secret of the manufacture of both plaques and mortar with him to his grave, but a number of his plaques can be seen in churchyards at Ashburnham, Brightling, Burwash, Cade Street, Chiddingly, East Hoathly, Glynde, Hailsham, Hellingly, Herstmonceux, Salehurst, Wadhurst, Waldron and Warbleton, as well as All Saint's churchyard in Heathfield. There is also an exhibition about the Harmer terracottas in the Anne of Cleves House museum in Lewes.

The area around Brightling, east of Heathfield, is famous for a number of follies built in the early 19th century by John 'Mad Jack' Fuller (1757-1834), an eccentric local squire and ironmaster who lived at the Rose Hill estate, now Brightling Park. These include the Obelisk (or Brightling Needle) on Brightling Down, built to commemorate the Battle of Waterloo in 1815, and the cone-shaped Sugar Loaf (or Fuller's Point) that stands in a field north of the B2056 just east of Woods Corner, south-west of Brightling, which Fuller is said to have built to win a bet. The story goes that he made a wager with a friend in London that he could see the spire of St Giles Church at Dallington from his house, but when he got home he found the view of the spire was blocked by a hill. Nothing daunted, in order to win the bet he had the Sugar Loaf folly built as a spire look-alike on high ground between his home and Dallington, which accurately resembled a distant view of the church's distinctive spire when seen from his house. He was delighted with his ploy, and claimed that 'no one can tell one from t'other'.

WADHURST, HIGH STREET 1903 49365

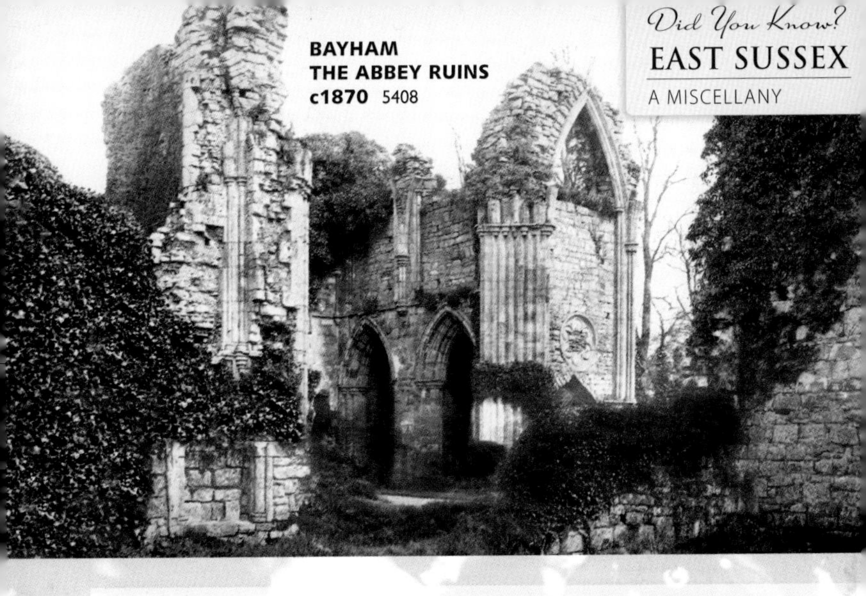

BAYHAM THE ABBEY RUINS c1870 5408

An important centre of the Sussex iron industry of the past was Wadhurst. The church of St Peter and St Paul in Wadhurst is famous for the large number of decorative cast-iron tomb slabs set into the floor, more than any other church in England; there are over thirty of these memorials, dating from between 1617 and 1790, many of which commemorate members of the Barham family who were important local ironmasters and landowners in the past.

North of Wadhurst, in the valley of the River Teise right on the East Sussex/Kent border, are the lovely ruins of Bayham Abbey, which was founded around 1207 as a house for Premonstratensian canons (the 'white canons'). Bayham Abbey was one of the few monastic houses that was not dissolved by Henry VIII in the 1530s as part of his religious changes, but was in fact closed down some years earlier, in 1525, by Cardinal Wolsey, the king's chancellor and advisor, as one of a number of religious houses he dissolved so he could transfer their endowments to the colleges he was founding at Oxford and his home town of Ipswich. These are the most impressive monastic remains in East Sussex, and are now in the care of English Heritage.

SPORTING EAST SUSSEX

An annual event in Brighton's calendar is The Royal Escape Yacht Race from Brighton to Fécamp on the Normandy coast of France, a distance of 67 nautical miles. The yacht race is organized by the Sussex Yacht Club and commemorates the escape to France from the Sussex coast of Prince Charles, later Charles II, following his defeat at the Battle of Worcester in 1651. Charles made his way across the country in disguise and eventually reached Brighton (then called Brighthelmstone), where his companions found someone willing to take them to France, Nicholas Tattersall, the captain of a coal brig called the 'Surprise' moored at Southwick. Charles returned in 1660 when he was restored to the throne as Charles II, and rewarded Captain Tattersall with an annuity which he used to buy the Ship Tavern in Brighthelmstone – now the Old Ship Hotel on King's Road in Brighton. The Royal Escape Yacht Race began in 1976 and is now a well-established part of the Sussex sailing calendar. The race starts just off Brighton Pier and is the largest offshore race on the South Coast outside the Solent, attracting a large mixed fleet of many kinds of sailing craft.

Hove is the home of Sussex County Cricket Club, which was formed in 1839 and is the oldest constituted county cricket club in the country; this also makes it the world's oldest first class cricket club. The County Cricket Ground famously has one of the truest pitches in England, and is one of the few county grounds to have deckchairs for spectators – which are in the traditional colours of Sussex County Cricket Club, blue and white.

The Bat and Trap pub in Ditchling Road in Brighton takes its name from the old game of Bat and Trap which used to be played on The Level opposite the pub on Good Friday morning, and is still played in Brighton occasionally. The pub has two signs, and the picture on the sign in Ditchling Road depicts the game in the pub's name, a bat-and-ball game played between two teams of up to eight players in which the ball is thrown into the air by the trap, a seesaw-like catapault, when the batsman hits the raised end of the trap with his bat. The batsman then attempts to hit the ball between two posts at the other end of the pitch. The other sign on the Bat and Trap pub, showing a cricketer, is a reminder of the time in the 1980s when the pub was called the Lords Bar, giving it a cricketing connection because The Level was once the site of Brighton's cricket ground.

Another ancient game that is still played in the county is Stoolball, which originated in Sussex in the 15th century and is played at local league level by a number of stoolball clubs in both East and West Sussex. It is played mainly by women and is similar to cricket. The two wickets, square boards 4 feet (1.22 metres) off the ground, are defended using round bats. Its name seems to come from its origins as a game played by milkmaids who used their milking stools as bats with another bat hung in a hedge or from a tree as the wicket. Despite its early origins, stoolball was only officially recognised as a sport by the Sports Council in 2008.

The only professional League Football club in East Sussex is Brighton & Hove Albion FC, founded in 1901. The club is nicknamed 'The Seagulls', or 'Albion'. A great moment in the Seagull's history was reaching the FA Cup final in 1983 in which they held Manchester United to a 2-2 draw, although they lost the replay five days later. More recent honours include winning the League One championship in the 2010-11 season.

A famous sporting event in East Sussex is the Eastbourne International tennis tournament held at the Devonshire Park Lawn Tennis Club, which has been held in the town since 1974. The Eastbourne International is attended by top international players as a warm-up to the Wimbledon tournament which begins the following week, because of its excellent grass courts – they are keen to practise on the unfamiliar surface, as Wimbledon is now the only Grand Slam tournament still played on grass. The Eastbourne International used to be a women-only tournament, but since 2009 but men have played there as well.

QUIZ QUESTIONS

Answers on page 52.

1. By what collective name are the coastal features of Haven Brow, Short Brow, Rough Brow, Bran Point, Flagstaff Point, Bailey's Hill and West Hill Brow better known?

2. Robertsbridge in East Sussex (off the A21 north of Battle) is famous for which items of sporting equipment made there?

3. Photograph 71427, opposite, shows the 14th-century half-timbered thatched Wealden hall house at Alfriston, west of Eastbourne, which is known as The Old Clergy House. It was originally built as a home for local priests, and in later centuries it was lived in by farm labourers. The house is famous for being the first building in the country to be bought by which organisation?

4. Which famous building in East Sussex was disparagingly described by William Cobbett (1763-1835) as a combination of 'a square box, a large Norfolk turnip and four onions'?

5. Which James Bond film features a burning Landrover driving off Beachy Head near Eastbourne?

6. St Leonard's Church at St Leonards-on-Sea, west of Hastings, has a most unusual pulpit – what is it?

7. How is it possible to stand in Peacehaven, on the East Sussex coast, with a foot in both the eastern and western hemispheres?

8. Whereabouts in East Sussex is the Cuckoo Trail, and what is it?

9. In June 2012 the nation celebrated the Diamond Jubilee of Queen Elizabeth II – 60 years on the throne. Only one other monarch in British history has celebrated a Diamond Jubilee, and that was Queen Victoria in 1897. Queen Victoria's Diamond Jubilee was commemorated at Westmeston, north-west of Lewes, with a landscape feature that can still be seen – what is it?

10. A 'looker' is an old East Sussex term for which occupation?

ALFRISTON, THE OLD CLERGY HOUSE 1921 71427

RECIPE

SUSSEX HEAVIES

These small, fruity cakes were originally made with the pastry left over from the weekly baking, with some dried fruit kneaded into the dough, and given to children as snacks. These are best eaten on the same day as baking, and are especially nice eaten hot, straight from the oven. This should make about 12 Heavies.

225g/8oz self-raising flour
A pinch of salt
25g/1oz caster sugar
50g/2oz butter or margarine
50g/2oz currants or raisins, or a mixture of both
175ml/6fl oz sour milk, or fresh milk 'soured' with the juice of half a lemon
A little extra caster sugar to finish

Pre-heat the oven to 220°C/425°F/Gas Mark 7 and grease a baking sheet.

Mix the flour, salt and sugar in a bowl. Rub in the butter or margarine until the mixture resembles fine breadcrumbs, then mix in the dried fruit. Mix to a soft dough with as much of the liquid as is necessary (reserve the rest).

Roll out the dough gently on a floured surface to about 2.5cms (1 inch) thick, and cut it into rounds about 5cms (2 inches) in diameter. Place the rounds on greased baking sheets, brush with the remaining sour milk and sprinkle with a little extra caster sugar. Bake near the top of the pre-heated oven for about 10 minutes, until golden brown.

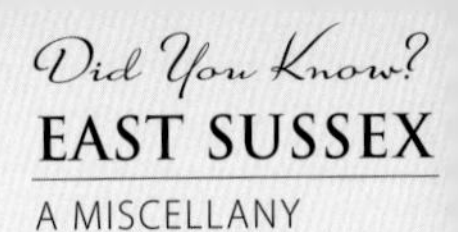

RECIPE

SUSSEX POND PUDDING

It used to be a Sussex tradition to eat this delicious pudding on Palm Sunday (the Sunday before Easter). It is filled with a sweet, buttery sauce, with a lemon hidden inside. When the pudding is cut open, the sauce spills out around it onto the serving dish like a pond.

225g/8oz self-raising flour
115g/4oz grated suet
50-75ml/2-3 fl oz milk
150g/5oz unsalted butter, cut small pieces
150g/5oz demerara sugar
1 large unwaxed lemon, washed and pricked deeply all over, right through the rind, with a fork or skewer

Sift the flour into a bowl. Add the suet and milk and mix to a dough. Roll out three-quarters of the dough and line a well-buttered 900ml (1½ pint) pudding basin. Put half the butter pieces into the pudding basin. Add half the sugar. Press one end of the lemon into the butter and sugar mixture, standing it upright. Press the remaining butter and sugar around and over the lemon. Fold the ends of pastry in over the filling and brush with a little water. Roll out the remaining pastry to make a lid and place on top of the pudding, pressing the edge to seal. Cover the basin with a lid of pleated kitchen foil (to allow room for expansion during cooking), buttered on the pudding side, and tie down firmly with string. Place the basin in a large saucepan filled with boiling water to halfway up its side, cover the pan with its lid and steam the pudding for 3½-4 hours, adding more boiling water when necessary so the pan doesn't boil dry. Lift the basin from the pan, remove the foil and carefully invert the pudding onto a deep serving dish, large enough to catch the lemony sauce as the pudding is cut open. Serve with custard, cream or lemon sauce, adding a piece of the lemon to each helping.

QUIZ ANSWERS

1. Haven Brow, Short Brow, Rough Brow, Bran Point, Flagstaff Point, Bailey's Hill and West Hill Brow are the individual names of the Seven Sisters, the seven dramatic chalk cliffs that undulate along the coast between Cuckmere Haven, east of Seaford, and Beachy Head. The depressions between the cliffs are the valleys of ancient rivers that used to run to the sea.

2. Cricket bats. The Gray-Nicolls company at Robertsbridge makes some of the best cricket bats in the world, using the wood of locally-grown willow trees.

3. In 1896 The Old Clergy House at Alfriston was the first property bought by the recently formed National Trust, which paid £10 for the building, but then spent a further £300 restoring it.

4. The Royal Pavilion at Brighton. It was also disliked by the Reverend Sydney Smith (1771-1845), curate of St Paul's Cathedral in London, who said it looked as if the dome of St Paul's 'had come to Brighton and pupped'.

5. 'The Living Daylights'.

6. The pulpit of St Leonard's Church in St Leonards-on-Sea is made from the prow of a boat brought from the Sea of Galilee in Israel.

7. In 1884 the line of longitude that passes through Greenwich Observatory in south-east London was chosen as the prime meridian, dividing the world into the eastern and western hemispheres. This meridian line passes through Peacehaven, and its position is marked by the Meridian Monument that stands on longitude zero on the cliff above the beach. There, as at Greenwich, it is possible to stand with one foot in the eastern hemisphere and the other in the western!

8. The Cuckoo Trail is a footpath and cycleway that runs from Hampden Park, north of Eastbourne, to Heathfield, largely following the route of the Cuckoo Line, a disused railway line that ran between Eridge Station and Polegate. The railway line was named after the Heffle Cuckoo Fair which still takes place at Heathfield every April and traditionally marks the beginning of spring.

9. On an escarpment of the north flank of the South Downs between Plumpton and Westmeston, north-west of Lewes (National Grid reference TQ 348 130) is a plantation of oak trees going up and down each side of a cleft in the Downs in the shape of a V. This was planted in celebration of Queen Victoria's Diamond Jubilee.

10. 'Looker' is an old Sussex term for a shepherd.

WESTDEAN, A SHEPHERD WITH HIS FLOCK 1922 71400

FRANCIS FRITH

PIONEER VICTORIAN PHOTOGRAPHER

Francis Frith, founder of the world-famous photographic archive, was a complex and multi-talented man. A devout Quaker and a highly successful Victorian businessman, he was philosophical by nature and pioneering in outlook. By 1855 he had already established a wholesale grocery business in Liverpool, and sold it for the astonishing sum of £200,000, which is the equivalent today of over £15,000,000. Now in his thirties, and captivated by the new science of photography, Frith set out on a series of pioneering journeys up the Nile and to the Near East.

INTRIGUE AND EXPLORATION

He was the first photographer to venture beyond the sixth cataract of the Nile. Africa was still the mysterious 'Dark Continent', and Stanley and Livingstone's historic meeting was a decade into the future. The conditions for picture taking confound belief. He laboured for hours in his wicker dark-room in the sweltering heat of the desert, while the volatile chemicals fizzed dangerously in their trays. Back in London he exhibited his photographs and was 'rapturously cheered' by members of the Royal Society. His reputation as a photographer was made overnight.

VENTURE OF A LIFE-TIME

By the 1870s the railways had threaded their way across the country, and Bank Holidays and half-day Saturdays had been made obligatory by Act of Parliament. All of a sudden the working man and his family were able to enjoy days out, take holidays, and see a little more of the world.

With typical business acumen, Francis Frith foresaw that these new tourists would enjoy having souvenirs to commemorate their days out. For the next thirty years he travelled the country by train and by pony and trap, producing fine photographs of seaside resorts and beauty spots that were keenly bought by millions of Victorians. These prints were painstakingly pasted into family albums and pored over during the dark nights of winter, rekindling precious memories of summer excursions. Frith's studio was soon supplying retail shops all over the country, and by 1890 F Frith & Co had become the greatest specialist photographic publishing company in the world, with over 2,000 sales outlets, and pioneered the picture postcard.

FRANCIS FRITH'S LEGACY

Francis Frith had died in 1898 at his villa in Cannes, his great project still growing. By 1970 the archive he created contained over a third of a million pictures showing 7,000 British towns and villages.

Frith's legacy to us today is of immense significance and value, for the magnificent archive of evocative photographs he created provides a unique record of change in the cities, towns and villages throughout Britain over a century and more. Frith and his fellow studio photographers revisited locations many times down the years to update their views, compiling for us an enthralling and colourful pageant of British life and character.

We are fortunate that Frith was dedicated to recording the minutiae of everyday life. For it is this sheer wealth of visual data, the painstaking chronicle of changes in dress, transport, street layouts, buildings, housing and landscape that captivates us so much today, offering us a powerful link with the past and with the lives of our ancestors.

Computers have now made it possible for Frith's many thousands of images to be accessed almost instantly. The archive offers every one of us an opportunity to examine the places where we and our families have lived and worked down the years. Its images, depicting our shared past, are now bringing pleasure and enlightenment to millions around the world a century and more after his death.

For further information visit: www.francisfrith.com

INTERIOR DECORATION

Frith's photographs can be seen framed and as giant wall murals in thousands of pubs, restaurants, hotels, banks, retail stores and other public buildings throughout Britain. These provide interesting and attractive décor, generating strong local interest and acting as a powerful reminder of gentler days in our increasingly busy and frenetic world.

FRITH PRODUCTS

All Frith photographs are available as prints and posters in a variety of different sizes and styles. In the UK we also offer a range of other gift and stationery products illustrated with Frith photographs, although many of these are not available for delivery outside the UK – see our web site for more information on the products available for delivery in your country.

THE INTERNET

Over 100,000 photographs of Britain can be viewed and purchased on the Frith web site. The web site also includes memories and reminiscences contributed by our customers, who have personal knowledge of localities and of the people and properties depicted in Frith photographs. If you wish to learn more about a specific town or village you may find these reminiscences fascinating to browse. Why not add your own comments if you think they would be of interest to others? See **www.francisfrith.com**

PLEASE HELP US BRING FRITH'S PHOTOGRAPHS TO LIFE

Our authors do their best to recount the history of the places they write about. They give insights into how particular towns and villages developed, they describe the architecture of streets and buildings, and they discuss the lives of famous people who lived there. But however knowledgeable our authors are, the story they tell is necessarily incomplete.

Frith's photographs are so much more than plain historical documents. They are living proofs of the flow of human life down the generations. They show real people at real moments in history; and each of those people is the son or daughter of someone, the brother or sister, aunt or uncle, grandfather or grandmother of someone else. All of them lived, worked and played in the streets depicted in Frith's photographs.

We would be grateful if you would give us your insights into the places shown in our photographs: the streets and buildings, the shops, businesses and industries. Post your memories of life in those streets on the Frith website: what it was like growing up there, who ran the local shop and what shopping was like years ago; if your workplace is shown tell us about your working day and what the building is used for now. Read other visitors' memories and reconnect with your shared local history and heritage. With your help more and more Frith photographs can be brought to life, and vital memories preserved for posterity, and for the benefit of historians in the future.

Wherever possible, we will try to include some of your comments in future editions of our books. Moreover, if you spot errors in dates, titles or other facts, please let us know, because our archive records are not always completely accurate—they rely on 140 years of human endeavour and hand-compiled records. You can email us using the contact form on the website.

Thank you!

For further information, trade, or author enquiries
please contact us at the address below:

**The Francis Frith Collection, Oakley Business Park,
Wylye Road, Dinton, Wiltshire SP3 5EU.**

Tel: +44 (0)1722 716 376 Fax: +44 (0)1722 716 881
e-mail: sales@francisfrith.co.uk **www.francisfrith.com**